Practical Project Stakeholder Management

Methods, Tools and Templates for Comprehensive Stakeholder Management

Emanuela Giangregorio

2nd Edition

Copyright

Copyright © Emanuela Giangregorio 2020. All rights reserved with the exception of the Permission Given below.

Permission Given: The author of this book gives purchasers express permission to copy the templates shown in this book and to use these for their own purposes.

Templates are denoted by this symbol:

This book is intended to provide practical guidance to its readers. The author expressly disclaims all liability to any person arising directly or indirectly from the use of, or for any errors or omissions in, the information in this book. The adoption and application of the of the information in this book is at the reader's discretion and is their sole responsibility.

Practical Project Stakeholder Management

First Edition Published in 2016

Author: Emanuela Giangregorio

Other Books by this Author

Practical Project Management

Practical Remote Team Leadership

OFFER

Would you like a complete set of Project Stakeholder Management templates you can use immediately without the hassle of recreating them?

If YES, please write a review of this book on your purchase platform. Email me a link to your review and I will email you all the templates in Word and Excel, which can easily be used in Google Docs and Sheets if preferred.

Email: emanuela@aikaizen.com

It has been said that "beauty is in the eye of the beholder".

So is project success!

Contents

1| Introduction to Project Stakeholder Management 1
   Tools and Templates for You to Use 1
   Importance of Project Stakeholder Management 2
   Definition of Project Stakeholder Management .. 3
   Definition of Project Stakeholders 4
   Chapter 1 Key Points 6

2| The Project Stakeholder Management Lifecycle 7
   Four Key Steps in the Life Cycle 7
   The Stakeholder Management Life Cycle 10
   Chapter 2 Key Points 13

3| Identifying your Project Stakeholders 14
   Who Are your Stakeholders ? 14
   Chapter 3 Key Points 17

4| Assessing Project Stakeholders 18
   Stakeholder Mapping 18
   Stakeholder Assessment Table 27
   Chapter 4 Key Points 29

5| Understanding Stakeholder Value Drivers 30
   Stakeholder Value Mapping 30
   Meeting with Key Stakeholders to Discuss their Expectations 33
   Recording Stakeholder Engagement Actions ... 35
   Chapter 5 Key Points 38

6|	Engaging your Stakeholders 39
	Stakeholder Communication Planning 39
	Using a RACI Matrix 43
	PARIS Matrix 46
	Stakeholder Assessment Frequency 46
	Showing a Stakeholder Mapping Over Time 46
	Chapter 6 Key Points 48
7|	Evaluating Stakeholder Management Effectiveness 49
	What to Cover in a Review 49
	Chapter 7 Key Points 52
8|	Ten Best Practices for Effective Project Stakeholder Management 53
	Concluding Remarks 55

1| Introduction to Project Stakeholder Management

Tools and Templates for You to Use

I have provided a number of tools and templates in this book, including some worked examples where relevant. If you are skim-reading through the book just to see the templates, look for this symbol:

Tools and Templates in this Book:

1. Influence-Involvement Grid
2. Influence-Involvement Grid Showing Level of Interest
3. Influence-Involvement Grid Showing Interest and Impact
4. Influence-Involvement Grid Showing Interest, Impact and Support
5. Stakeholder Resistance Mapping
6. Stakeholder Assessment Table Example
7. Stakeholder Value Mapping Example
8. Project Stakeholder Engagement Meeting Agenda Example
9. Stakeholder Engagement Template – Worked Example

10. Project Stakeholder Expectations Alignment Template
11. Project Stakeholder Communication Plan Template
12. Project Stakeholder Communication Plan Example
13. RACI Matrix Example
14. Stakeholder Mapping Across Stages
15. Stakeholder Management Effectiveness Review Template

Depending on the device you are using to read this book, you may need to increase the image size to see the detail clearly.

Importance of Project Stakeholder Management

One of the most challenging aspects on projects is managing stakeholder expectations and getting their commitment and buy-in to the project. Many project failures are attributed to the lack of stakeholder involvement in, and support of, the project. Quite often, we involve our stakeholders too late in the project process, or even worse... some are left out completely until things go wrong. On the other hand, when we do involve our stakeholders, they are sometimes not engaged in the process. Sometimes we have the opposite extreme – they get "too involved" and slow us down.

Project Stakeholder Management is one of the key processes in most project methodologies. As we are dealing with people, it is more art than science. When you effectively manage your project stakeholders, you build relationships, engagement and collaboration - key ingredients to project success.

Definition of Project Stakeholder Management

So how is "Project Stakeholder Management" defined ? My definition of Project Stakeholder Management is as follows:

*"Project Stakeholder Management is one of a number of **project management processes** that takes place throughout the project lifecycle, to **identify, assess and engage** project stakeholders in a manner that leads to **maximised collaboration in support of project success.**"*

This definition embodies three key aspects of stakeholder management:

1. Project Stakeholder Management is a *process*, not a one-off activity performed at the start of the project. Anyone that has delivered several projects will have had the repeated experience that the challenge on projects is not mostly with the solution being delivered, but the people involved (or that should be involved) in the process. Different stakeholders will have different levels of significance to the project at different stages of the project. A good Project Manager will assess the stakeholders at key points throughout the project lifecycle and will have proactive plans to secure their buy-in and engagement.
2. There are a number of *steps in the process*, including identifying the stakeholders, assessing the stakeholders and engaging them in the project. I will demonstrate exactly how to do this in later

chapters, and share with you the tools and templates that you can use going forward.

3. The primary purpose of taking a proactive approach to Project Stakeholder Management is to *maximise collaboration* on the project, as this will go a long way to support project success.

Definition of Project Stakeholders

How broad is the group of project stakeholders? When we talk about "project stakeholders", who exactly do we mean ? To make it simple to remember, I use the "4 I" definition. Project Stakeholders are the group of people that:

1. Are Involved in the project, and/or
2. Have a vested Interest in the project, and/or
3. Can Influence the project, and/or
4. Are Impacted by the project.

The "stake" that each of these individuals or groups has in a project, will vary. For example, in a system implementation project for the Sales division of a company, the Supply Chain Director may not be influential on the project, involved in the project or impacted by the project. But she may be *interested* in the project, as this may be a system she is considering for her division later.

There will be overlaps in your list of stakeholders across these 4 I's. For example, in the system implementation project for the Sales division referred to above, the Sales Director could be involved, interested, influential and impacted. My 4I definition is useful when you are listing all your project stakeholders. Once done, ask yourself (or the team if in a workshop), have I thought of all the individuals and groups that are involved, interested, influential and impacted ? This way, you get a broader and more comprehensive list of project stakeholders.

Remember also that for many projects, the group of stakeholders could vary as the project proceeds. Hence, for longer projects, there is a need for the Project Manager to refresh their stakeholder identification and analysis throughout the project life cycle.

Rule: Focus on Understanding the Spirit of the Method

In the chapters that follow, I will explain how to go about project stakeholder management on projects. Please bear in mind that the tools and techniques I share with you are *scaleable in their application*.

For example, if you are managing a 2-year construction project – say a new block of apartments is being built next to a school - you would be expected to perform regular and robust stakeholder management throughout the project, and would probably want to use the templates provided here to assist you in the process.

On a simpler 2-month project – say to organise your division's annual team building event - you would only be expected to implement the spirit of the method.

As you progress through the Chapters in this book, ensure you understand the *spirit* of the method. Ask yourself, "What is the essence of the technique ? What is the purpose of performing that particular assessment ?" Once you understand the spirit of the method, you can then apply it accordingly to suit the nature and complexity of your projects.

Chapter 1 Key Points

- Importance of Project Stakeholder Management
- Definition of Project Stakeholder Management
- Definition of Project Stakeholders – the 4 I's.
- Ensure you understand the spirit of the method

oooOooo

2| The Project Stakeholder Management Lifecycle

In this chapter, I will summarise each of the steps in the stakeholder management lifecycle, and will show where this lifecycle fits in the project management lifecycle. I will elaborate on each of the techniques and supporting tools for each stage in subsequent chapters.

Four Key Steps in the Life Cycle

1. Identify Stakeholders

The first stage is the stakeholder *identification* stage. We cannot manage the stakeholders unless we know who they are. In this stage, we would list all the individuals and groups that are involved, interested, influential and impacted by the project.

In shorter, less complex projects, this would be a one-off exercise early on in the project. On longer, more complex projects, the Project Manager would want to refresh the list of stakeholders periodically throughout the project. This should be performed as you approach the end of a key project stage. For example, in an 18 month construction project that is approaching the end of the Design stage, the list of stakeholders should be refreshed and assessed before continuing on to the Build stage. If you are familiar with the "Stage Gate" approach in project management, then this is one of the actions that would be performed at each stage gate.

2. Assess Stakeholders

The list of stakeholders you identify could be an overwhelmingly long list. It is therefore important to segment our pack of stakeholders so that we can prioritise them, and focus the way we engage them.

In the *stakeholder assessment* stage, we need to know:
- How involved are they in the project?
- What is their interest in the project?
- How influential are they on the project?
- To what extent are they impacted by the project?

We also need to know what is their level of support, or buy-in, to the project. Additionally, it would be useful to know what they value – in other words, what is important to them in the context of the project – and to have a good idea whether they have realistic expectations of the project.

As you will may have gathered, there is a lot to the assessment stage. On short, uncomplicated projects, you would apply a very simple version of this assessment. Once you have listed the project stakeholders, you merely need to consider the nature of their involvement, level of support and their expectations of the project.

On large, complex projects with many different types of stakeholders, you are likely to identify individuals and groups with vastly differing levels of involvement and support, along with divergent needs and expectations. A thorough analysis in this case is therefore crucial. If you don't have a good understanding of your stakeholders, it will be very difficult to proactively manage their engagement on the project.

3. Engage Stakeholders

Once we have assessed the project stakeholders, we can establish how we will engage them on the project and when. A one-size-fits-all solution will not necessarily be appropriate, as different stakeholders will have a different "stake" in the project. We use the output of our assessment to develop a robust and workable Stakeholder Engagement Plan. This includes when we meet with them, what and how we communicate with them, and how we can proactively foster their support of the project. In large projects, you can expect to have different groups of stakeholders to engage at different stages of the project.

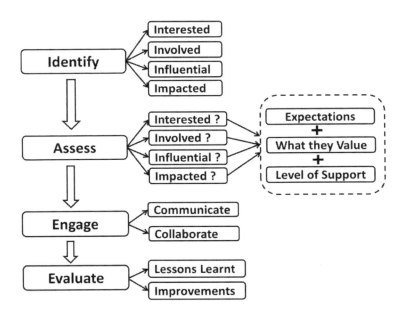

4. Evaluate Effectiveness

Finally, at the end of the project, it is a good practice to evaluate the effectiveness of our stakeholder management process.

This can be done as part of the "lessons learnt" exercise typically performed during the project closure stage. On longer projects, I recommend you do this towards the end of each stage or at key milestones. In this exercise, you will discuss and document the aspects of your stakeholder management that was performed well, and which aspects would benefit from improvement on future projects, or for the rest of your current project if performing an interim review.

The Stakeholder Management Life Cycle

I will explain what is involved in each of the above steps in more detail later. First, let's look at where the stakeholder management life cycle fits in with the project life cycle.

Consider a simple project management life cycle comprising four project phases: Initiation, Definition, Execution and Close. If you are not familiar with the activities in each of the phases, or what is meant by the Stage Gate approach, please read my book "Practical Project Management Principles".

We can identify project stakeholders as early as the Initiation phase. It may well be those that are the most influential and impacted that would need to be consulted during the initiation phase, before getting into the detailed planning of the project in the Definition phase.

Once you have a good idea of the project scope, objectives and key milestones in the Definition phase, you can then prepare a more comprehensive list of project stakeholders. However, just as project planning (definition) continues during project execution in many projects, you may also identify new stakeholders well into the execution phase. This is particularly true of projects which have a long duration.

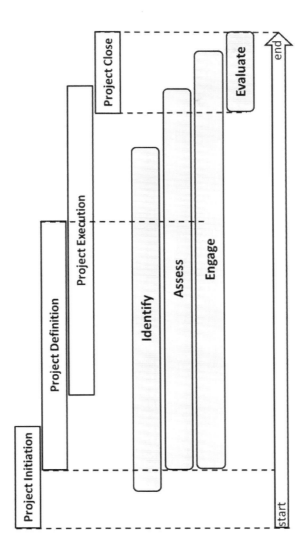

Once you have identified the stakeholders, you will assess them to work out the best way to engage them throughout the project. Achieving stakeholder engagement means getting their appropriate involvement, commitment and buy-in to the project. So for a project to be successful, some key stakeholders will need to be engaged as early on as possible in the project, while others will only need to be engaged later on in the project life cycle.

Like many other project management activities, your stakeholder management activity should be planned, actioned, tracked and evaluated. If you are managing a medium to large project, I highly recommend you integrate stakeholder management as a *specific activity* on your project. Very large projects will actually have a Stakeholder Engagement Manager.

Remember: The spirit of project stakeholder management is to obtain the optimal level of stakeholder engagement in support of project success. In my experience, for stakeholder management to be effective in its support of project success, it should be a priority process that spans the entire project life cycle. How you go about it will depend on the nature and complexity of your project.

Chapter 2 Key Points

- Summary of the four key steps in the Project Stakeholder Management Lifecycle
- How and why the Project Stakeholder Management Lifecycle spans most of the Project Lifecycle

oooOooo

3| Identifying your Project Stakeholders

As mentioned previously, the project stakeholders are not only those people that are involved in the project. They are also those that have a vested interest in the project, that are influential on the project, and that are impacted by the project. A stakeholder could have one, or a combination of all of these "I" associations with the project.

Who Are your Stakeholders ?

When you consider those that are *impacted*, you need to think of those that are impacted *during* the project and those that would be impacted *after* the project. For example, in an office move project, some people who are not involved in the move may be impacted by disruption caused by the office move *during* the project. Once the move has taken place and the project is closed, there may be those that are impacted afterwards, for example, people that used to have an office now have to sit in open plan office configuration. Another example of those impacted after the project is if the new location of the office means that some people have to travel a longer distance to work.

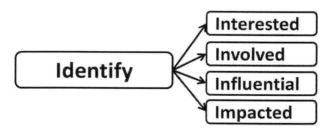

When we talk about those stakeholders that are *influential*, we mean those individuals or groups that could positively or negatively impact the project. For example, a workers union could be influential if they have the power to stop a project through legal action. The Project Sponsor is also influential as he should have the power to approve additional budget for scope changes.

On large projects, you could have a very long list of stakeholders, so it is a good practice to segment them first into those that are internal to the project, those that are internal to the organisation, and those that are external to the organisation.

In some cases, we would need to manage individual stakeholders (e.g. Head of Marketing) and in other cases, we would manage an entire group of stakeholders (e.g. customers). List individuals by name or Job Title so that everybody on the project knows who you are talking about.

You may have an individual who is also part of a group, and you may want to manage them separately. For example, in an office move project, the Head of Facilities Management would be an individual that you would want to engage with as he is key to the project. However, he is also part of the group of people ("Office Staff") that will be moving to the new offices.

Practical Project Stakeholder Management

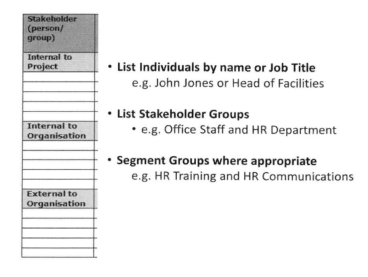

- **List Individuals by name or Job Title**
  e.g. John Jones or Head of Facilities

- **List Stakeholder Groups**
  - e.g. Office Staff and HR Department

- **Segment Groups where appropriate**
  e.g. HR Training and HR Communications

Typically, when you are identifying your project stakeholders, you would meet with the core project team to discuss and identify those individuals and groups that are project stakeholders. For completeness, it is useful to refer to a Project Stakeholder Checklist or even a current organisation chart (for internal stakeholders).

When considering those that are *external* to the organisation, you need to consider not only suppliers to the project, but also any other third parties such as government bodies, regulatory agencies, the media or customers.

|16

Chapter 3 Key Points

- When listing stakeholders that will be impacted by the project, consider those that will be impacted *during* and *after* the project.

- If you have a long list of stakeholders, segment the list into those that are internal to the project, those that are internal to the organisation, and those that are external to the organisation.

- Separate individual stakeholders from the group if that individual is significantly differently involved, impacted, influential or interested.

- Your stakeholders may be similar across similar projects. Use a Project Stakeholder Checklist or current organisation chart for completeness and to save time.

oooOooo

Practical Project Stakeholder Management

4| Assessing Project Stakeholders

In this chapter, I am going to show you a fairly rigorous approach to assessing your project stakeholders. Remember that this approach is *scalable*. For small projects, the framework would merely prompt brief consideration, and for large projects you would follow this approach in more detail. There are two tools you can use: (i) a chart or (ii) a table. I will demonstrate the assessment process using the chart first, and then show you the tabular version which lends itself more to project documentation.

Stakeholder Mapping

First, we want to map our project stakeholders in terms of their level of *influence on the project* and level of *involvement in the project*.

Plot the stakeholders where you believe they fit in this 3x3 grid. For example, below is a stakeholder mapping showing a subset of stakeholders for an Office Move Project. The Leaseholder, Furniture Suppliers, Cleaners and Movers are external to the organisation.

Influence-Involvement Grid

Level of Influence on the Project				
high	Head of Trading Lease Holder	Health & Safety Mgr	Facilities Manager Head of IT
medium	Legal	Furniture Supplier	IT Help Desk Mgr Movers
low	Cleaners	General Office Staff	
	low	medium	high

Level of Involvement on the Project

Once you have mapped your stakeholders' level of influence and involvement, you should also show their level of *interest* in the project. When we consider their interest in the project, we consider how much they want to be kept appraised of project progress and project outcomes. For stakeholders that you have not engaged with yet, e.g. General Office Staff, you should anticipate their level of interest. For others, e.g. Head of Trading, you should obtain this early on through discussion with them.

Influence-Involvement Grid Showing Level of Interest

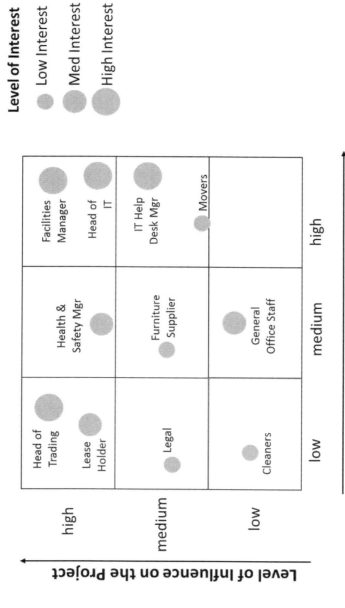

Practical Project Stakeholder Management

In the above example, our internal Legal team have a low interest in the project, as do the external suppliers. The Leaseholder has a medium level of interest as once we vacate the office they would want to occupy it with new tenants. So the Leaseholder would want to be kept appraised of project progress and any issues that would impact their objectives.

Next we can show how each of the stakeholders is *impacted* by the project – take a look at the next chart.

The Head of Facilities Management and his team have the greatest involvement in the project and are most impacted by the project in terms of their time and availability. The IT Help Desk Manager has also indicated that this office move will have a high impact on her and her team, as the Help Desk teams will need to be re-organised due to short-comings at the new facilities, plus they are expecting a high call volume following the move.

Influence-Involvement Grid Showing Interest and Impact

Practical Project Stakeholder Management

Level of Interest
- Low Interest
- Med Interest
- High Interest

Level Impacted
L = Low Impact
M = Med Impact
H = High Impact

	low	medium	high
high	Head of Trading (M); Lease Holder (M)	Health & Safety Mgr (L)	Facilities Manager (H); Head of IT (M)
medium	Legal (L)	Furniture Supplier (L)	IT Help Desk Mgr (H); Movers (L)
low	Cleaners (M)	General Office Staff (M)	

Level of Influence on the Project (vertical axis)
Level of Involvement in the Project (horizontal axis)

| 22

So far, we have mapped the stakeholders according to the four "I's": influence, involvement, interest and impact. But what about support ? Most projects result in change of some sort. Where there is change, you are likely to have stakeholders that are your "Change Champions" and those that are your "Change Resistors." In an office move project, we can expect some people will be supportive of the project, whereas others will be resisting the change. It depends on the *stake* for them, and whether they perceive they will be positively or negatively impacted. If you are expecting different levels of buy-in, you can use a colour coding to show the stakeholders' level of buy-in and support of the project as shown in the next chart.

Influence-Involvement Grid Showing Interest, Impact and Support

Practical Project Stakeholder Management

Level of Interest
○ Low Interest
◯ Med Interest
◯ High Interest

Level Impacted
L = Low Impact
M = Med Impact
H = High Impact

Level of Support
■ Low buy-in
■ Med buy-in
■ High buy-in

Level of Influence on the Project	low	medium	high
high	Facilities Manager (H), Head of IT (M)	Health & Safety Mgr (L)	Head of Trading (M), Lease Holder (M)
medium	IT Help Desk Mgr (H), Movers (L)	Furniture Supplier (L)	Legal (L)
low		General Office Staff (M)	Cleaners (M)

Level of Involvement in the Project →

| 24

Practical Project Stakeholder Management

In the above example, you have established that the Head of Trading is highly unsupportive of the project because he does not trust that the move will be successful from a technology and connectivity perspective, and is highly concerned about the impact this will have to business continuity. The IT Help Desk Manager has not bought in to the project because her team will now have less desk space at the new facilities and will have to be re-organised due a shortage of space for them. She knows this will affect their motivation and ability to work as well as they do at the current location. The Head of IT shares some concerns as do some of the general office staff that will be moving. The Cleaning company is not fully collaborative because the move on that weekend clashes with schedules they have for other clients.

Knowing where the resistance and support lies on your project is essential, as this will help you focus your stakeholder engagement efforts. In this example, your Engagement Plan should include 1:1 meetings with the Head of Trading and with the IT Help Desk Manager. All their concerns should be recorded and proactive risk management should be in place to allay their concerns.

An alternative chart is the one on the next page. On projects where you are expecting resistance to change, this is a better template as the focus here is on identifying levels of project support and developing tactics to maximise support (i.e. resolve and minimise resistance). Using this chart, my priority would be to work with the "Game Changers" to become "Champions". If my efforts as Project Manager fail, I can use the "Champions" to influence the "Game Changers". The "Cheer Leaders" are also important because they positively promote the project and could become more influential. Whilst the "Sceptics" are my lowest priority, I still want them on my radar in case their influence changes. The people that are undecided or do not care about the project are also a group that I want to understand because getting their support could help with swaying the "Game Changers" and "Sceptics".

Stakeholder Support Mapping

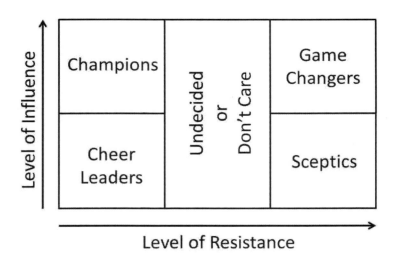

Practical Project Stakeholder Management

Stakeholder Assessment Table

Some project managers like to map out their stakeholders on charts similar to the ones I have shown above, as the charts provide a quick visual mapping of the stakeholders and a great basis for discussing the stakeholders with the core project team. Others prefer to record the information in a table similar to the Stakeholder Assessment template shown on the next page.

Here you can see the first 6 columns of the Stakeholder Assessment Template. The first column is the list of stakeholders, segmented by those internal to the project, internal to the organisation and external to the organisation. In the next 5 columns, you can use the same High, Medium and Low classification to indicate their level of interest, involvement, influence, impact and buy-in.

In the worked example shown, I have highlighted in red those players that have a low buy-in to the project, amber those that have a medium buy-in to the project, and green for those players that have a high support of the project (your reading device or print version of this book may not show these colours).

There are further columns in this table, and that is because our assessment is not complete yet. In the next chapter, I will explain about performing a Value Mapping to understand what is important to your stakeholders.

Stakeholder Assessment Table Example

| 27

Stakeholder Assessment

Stakeholder (person/group)	Level of Interest in Project (H/M/L)	Level of Involvement on Project (H/M/L)	Level of Influence on Project (H/M/L)	Level Impacted by project (H/M/L)	Level of Buy-in (Support) to project (H/M/L)
Internal to Project					
Head of Facilities	H	H	H	H	H
Head of IT	H	H	H	M	M
IT Help Desk Mgr	H	H	M	H	L
Health & Safety Mgr	M	M	H	L	H
Internal to Organisation					
Head of Trading	H	L	H	M	L
Legal	L	L	M	L	H
General office staff	M	M	L	M	M
External to Organisation					
Lease Holder	M	L	H	M	H
Furniture Supplier	L	M	M	L	H
Movers	L	H	M	L	H
Cleaners	L	L	L	M	M

Chapter 4 Key Points

- Use a chart or a table to assess your stakeholders in terms of their interest, involvement, influence, impact and level of support.
- If you are expecting resistance to your project, use the Influence-Resistance chart and a corresponding table.
- You would only be expected to perform this level of detailed analysis for large, complex projects so that you can prepare focused and proactive stakeholder engagement plans.
- For simpler projects, the framework would merely prompt consideration about each of your stakeholders. For example, on a 6-week project to create a department website, you could just list each of the stakeholders and indicate which are those that you need to manage more closely by considering the 4Is, and their level of buy-in to the project.

oooOooo

5| Understanding Stakeholder Value Drivers

To have a robust assessment of our stakeholders, we also need to know what is important to them – what they value – and whether their expectations are aligned with what the project intends deliver. Projects are successful if the scope is delivered on time, within budget and to the level of quality required.

However, you could deliver a project successfully "on paper", i.e. the documented scope was delivered to time, budget and quality requirements, BUT some stakeholders could be unhappy. Therefore, a project is only truly successful if key stakeholders deem it to be. To manage stakeholders effectively, we have to have a good grasp of *what is important to them in the context of the project* – sometimes called their *project value drivers*.

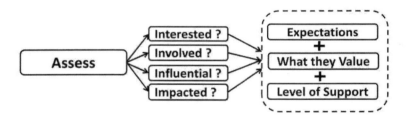

Stakeholder Value Mapping

There are different ways to perform a Stakeholder Value Mapping. I like to use a table such as the one below, in which we can show where there are similarities and differences between stakeholders regarding their project value drivers.

Stakeholder Value Mapping Example

The boxes marked in red (shaded in black and white versions of this book) show the one most important value driver for that stakeholder.

Ideally, you want to consult with the stakeholders to establish what is important to them. However, I fully understand that this is not always practical or appropriate, in which case you would need to make an educated guess about their value drivers.

Value mapping of this nature is an important exercise in stakeholder assessment. As you can see in the example, not everyone has the same needs. Stakeholder value mapping will help you, *not only* in your stakeholder engagement efforts, but *also* in project planning and risk management. The Value Drivers shown along the top are obtained from your discussions with the stakeholders and what you have picked up so far about their interest in the project.

Stakeholder Assessment – Value Mapping

Stakeholder (person/group)	Minimal Business Disruption	Comfortable work space	New work space better than previous	Same or less travel to work	Cheaper office space	No change to move date	Compliance with Regulations	Paid on time	IT Connectivity working without fault
Internal to Project									
Head of Facilities			x		x	x	x		x
Head of IT	x	x	x	x		x			x
IT Help Desk Mgr	x	x		x					x
Health & Safety Mgr		x					x		
Internal to Organisation									
Head of Trading	x	x	x	x		x			x
Legal		x	x	x			x		
General office staff	x	x	x						x
External to Organisation									
Lease Holder						x	x	x	
Furniture Supplier						x	x	x	
Movers						x	x	x	
Cleaners	x					x	x		

x (highlighted) = the one most important value driver for that stakeholder

Meeting with Key Stakeholders to Discuss their Expectations

When you meet with your key project stakeholders early on in the project, it's a good idea to have discussions with them, regarding *their expectations* of the project, *and what the project expects of them*.

In this discussion, you should also note their key concerns and level of buy-in to the project. In some cases you could meet with them as a group, and in other cases you would meet with them 1:1. On very large projects, the stakeholder consultation period could last several months.

Below is an example 10-point Agenda for a stakeholder meeting in a scenario where they are internal to the organisation. For example, in the Office Move Project, you could invite the Head of Facilities, Head of IT, IT Help Desk Manager, Health and Safety Manager and Head of Trading to one meeting. If you can't get them all together in one room/web meeting, you would need to meet with them individually. Separately you would consult with Legal, a Focus Group representing the Office Staff and the Leaseholder.

Agenda: Key Project Stakeholder Engagement Meeting

Purpose of the Meeting:

To ensure Stakeholder and Project expectations are aligned and understood, and to agree actions that will maximise project success.

Topics:

1. Project Objectives, Scope and Timelines
2. Project Roles and Responsibilities
3. Level of Interest in the Project (L/M/H)...why?
4. Level of Involvement in the Project (L/M/H)...why?
5. Level of Influence on the Project (L/M/H)...why?
6. How much are you impacted by the project...why?
7. Any issues/concerns you have about the Project
8. What you expect from the Project
9. What the Project expects from you
10. What is most important to you regarding this Project ?

Recording Stakeholder Engagement Actions

Once you have had your meetings and gathered all the stakeholder assessment information, you can summarise it in your Stakeholder Assessment Table, as shown on the next page. In the "Level of Buy-In" column, you can use red, amber and green shading for quick identification of those that are resisting the project (low buy-in). Alternative wording for this column heading would be "engagement".

Stakeholder Engagement Template – Worked Example

Let's be clear that the assessment stage is not just about filling in templates and charts... it's about getting a *good understanding* of your project stakeholders. You can then focus your planning, risk management and communication efforts on the project, in collaboration with your stakeholders.

Remember that the assessment processes, and supporting tools, are *scalable*. You might decide that the table on the next page is too detailed, and that your focus is not an analysis of influence, involvement etc. but purely on expectations management. In that case, use a simplified version like the one shown, headed "Stakeholder Expectations Alignment".

Practical Project Stakeholder Management

Stakeholder Assessment

Stakeholder (person/ group)	Level of Interest in Project (H/M/L)	Level of Involvement on Project (H/M/L)	Level of Influence on Project (H/M/L)	Level Impacted by project (H/M/L)	Level of Buy-in (Support) to project (H/M/L)	What they Expect of the Project	What the Project Expects of them	What they Value; What's Important to them**
Internal to Project								
Head of Facilities	H	H	H	H	H	• Weekly 1:1 status meeting • No surprises on issues	• Attend planning meetings • Staff availability • Attendance at Steering Committee meetings	Cheaper office space
Head of IT	H	H	H	M	M	• Monthly 1:1 status meeting	• IT Contingency Plan • Attendance at Steering Committee meetings	Minimal business disruption
IT Help Desk Mgr	H	H	M	H	L	• Involvement in project planning • Involvement in desk allocation	• Help Desk core team to be available 6am on first Monday following move	New work space better than previous
Health & Safety Mgr	H	M	H	L	H	• Communication on any H&S matter	• H&S full ownership and sign-off	Compliance with regulations
Internal to Organisation								
Head of Trading	H	L	H	M	L	• Proactive risk management • No move for Trading Desk unless 100% working • IT Contingency Plan	• Attendance at Steering Committee meetings	IT connectivity working faultless

**See Value Mapping for more detail on the last column; only most important value driver is included here

Project Stakeholder Expectations Alignment

Stakeholder (person or group)	What They expect from the Project	What the Project expects of Them	Agreed Actions

Chapter 5 Key Points

- Meet with your stakeholders to understand what is important to them in the context of the project.
- Use this opportunity to note their expectations of the project and to confirm what the project expects of them.
- Stakeholder assessment is not about competing templates and charts; it is about using these tools to have a structured approach to understanding the stakeholders of your project so that you can develop focused stakeholder engagement plans.

oooOooo

6| Engaging your Stakeholders

When you meet with your stakeholders to discuss the project as part of your stakeholder assessment, this already starts the engagement process. Two key ingredients for engagement are communication and collaboration.

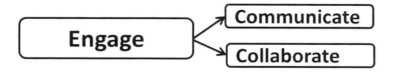

Stakeholder Communication Planning

On large projects, proactive Communication Planning is an essential project activity. The output of your Stakeholder Assessment is a key input to developing the Project Stakeholder Communication Plan.

Project Stakeholder Communication Plan Template

Project Stakeholder Communication Plan

Stakeholder (person/ group)	Meetings			Reports			
	Weekly status meeting	Monthly status meeting	Stage Gate meeting	Weekly Project Status	Monthly Highlight Report	Monthly newsletter	Exception Reports
Internal to Project							
Internal to Organisation							
External to Organisation							

Communication Channels:
- F2F = face-to-face
- TC = Teleconference
- VC = Video Conference
- PIP = Project Intranet Page
- e = Email

There are three key parts to this template:

- The left hand column is the list of stakeholders, segmented by those internal to the project, internal to the organisation and external to the organisation.

- The second part shows the *types of meetings* that will be held to discuss project progress and make decisions. In this example, we have weekly status meetings, monthly status meetings and project stage gate meetings.

- The third part shows the *scheduled project reporting*. In the above example, we have weekly project status reports, monthly highlight reports, a monthly project newsletter and exception reports.

It is fairly common nowadays for stakeholders to collaborate on projects from different locations. So it is important to show the channel of communication. In this example, we can have face-to-face, teleconference, video conference, a project intranet page and email communication.

In the office move project example here, you can see how the matrix is populated.

Project Stakeholder Communication Plan Example

Project Stakeholder Communication Plan

Stakeholder (person/group)	Meetings			Reports			
	Weekly status meeting	Monthly status meeting	Stage Gate meeting	Weekly Project Status	Monthly Highlight Report	Monthly newsletter	Exception Reports
Internal to Project							
Head of Facilities	F2F	F2F	F2F	X	X	X	X
Head of IT		TC	TC		X		X
IT Help Desk Mgr		F2F	F2F	X	X		X
Health & Safety Mgr		F2F	F2F		X		X
Internal to Organisation							
Head of Trading		F2F	F2F		X		X
Legal					X		
General office staff						X	
External to Organisation							
Lease Holder		as required					
Furniture Supplier		as required					
Movers		as required					
Cleaners		as required					

Communication Channels:
- F2F = face-to-face
- TC = Teleconference
- e = Email: All reports will be sent by email

Note that your Communication Plan reflects the *scheduled* meetings and reporting on the project. Of course, throughout the project, you will have ad-hoc meetings and status updates.

The primary aim of developing a Stakeholder Communication Plan is to ensure two things: (i)you consider all your stakeholders in your communication and (ii) you give the right people the right information they need on the project with the right frequency. For example, the Legal team or their project representative does not want to attend any of the meetings or receive any of the reports, with the exception of the monthly highlight report. Whilst we want to ensure we keep the stakeholders sufficiently appraised of progress and involved in project discussion, we also need to strike a balance. We do not want to over-involve them in meetings of low value to them, or send them reports that they will never read.

On longer projects, your communication is likely to change. I recommend checking your Communication Plan quarterly, or as you approach the end of a stage and start planning for the next stage.

Using a RACI Matrix

Another useful tool for confirming the degree of engagement relevant project stakeholders should have on the project, is the RACI matrix.

RACI Matrix Example

Project RACI Matrix

Stakeholder (person/group)	Primary Location	Project Planning	Key Decisions	Office layout	Workspace allocation	Office Move (packed boxes)	IT Cabling Installation	Telephony	IT Connectivity	Furniture installation
Internal to Project										
Project Manager	London	A, R	R, C, I	R	R	C, I	R	R	R	C, I
Project Board	London	I	R, A	C, I	C, I	I	I	I	I	I
Head of Facilities	UK	C, I	R, C, I	A	A, R	A	C, I	A, C, I	C, I	A
Head of IT	Leeds	C, I	R, C, I	C, I	C, I	I	A	I	A	C, I
IT Help Desk Mgr	Leeds	C, I	C, I	C, I	R, C, I	I	C, I	C, I	C, I	C, I
Health & Safety Mgr	London	C, I	C, I	C, I	C, I	C, I	C, I	C, I	C, I	C, I
Internal to Organisation										
Head of Trading	London	C, I	C, I	C, I	C, I	I	I	I	I	I
Legal	London	I	C, I	I	C, I					I
General office staff	UK	I	I	I	C, I	I				I
External to Organisation										
Current Lease Holder	London	I	I			I				I
Furniture Supplier	York	I	I	C	C					R
Movers	London	I	I			R				I
Cleaners	London	I	I			I				I

Responsible (responsible for doing the work)

Accountable (overall in charge, makes final decision and takes full ownership)

Consult (consulted for opinion and requirements through discussion)

Inform (advised of outcome)

The first column shows the stakeholders and the next column shows where they are located if not all in the same city. Along the top, from the third column onwards, we show the key project activity. Now this matrix is not comprehensive as I need to fit it in this book, but the example shows you the type of project activity you would include in order to clarify the nature of people's expected engagement on the project.

At the bottom is the RACI explanation:

- R is for "responsible" – this is the person/group that will actually perform the activity.

- A is for "accountable" – this is the person who is overall in charge, who makes the final decision and takes full ownership. In some organisations, the A is for Approve. Ideally we should have single accountability, but in some cases it would be a group of people, e.g. Project Board.

- C is for "consult" – this is the person/group we need to have a discussion with during the execution of the related project activity; their input is important.

- I is for "inform" – this is the person/group that needs to be advised of the outcome of the relevant project activity once it is completed.

It can be quite a lot of work creating a RACI matrix for your project. However, this level of detailed analysis is very useful when there is confusion or disagreement about roles and responsibilities, or how people need to interface with the project. In my experience, most people know who is responsible and accountable/approvers. Where things go wrong is when the right people are not consulted and informed (at all or at the right time). Having this matrix as a framework for assessments helps clarify how different roles need to be engaged in a project.

PARIS Matrix

Another version of the RACI matrix concept is the PARIS matrix:

- Participate
- Approve
- Responsible
- Inform
- Support

Stakeholder Assessment Frequency

Note that your assessment and supporting plans and documents are unlikely to be *static documents* throughout the project. On long projects, say any project that lasts for 9 months or more, you would probably review your Stakeholder Assessment and Communication Plan every three months or at appropriate stages of the project.

Showing a Stakeholder Mapping Over Time

When you chart the project stakeholders, you are showing their mapping at a point in time. If you are using the Influence-Involvement chart, you may want to show how their influence and involvement would change as the project moves from one stage to the next. This is useful to help visualise stakeholder activity on the project. See example on the next page.

Stakeholder Mapping Across Stages

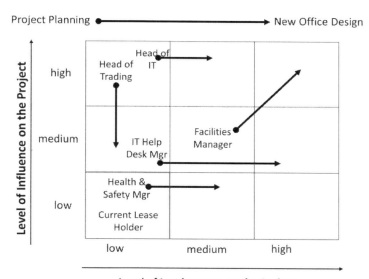

Chapter 6 Key Points

- Two key ingredients for stakeholder engagement are communication and collaboration.

- You can use the Stakeholder Communication Plan template to visualise how you are going to stay in touch with your stakeholders and with what frequency through which channel.

- If you are leading a complex project where there is confusion or disagreement about roles and responsibilities, the RACI matrix is useful. This matrix is also a prompt to ensure we don't forget to consult and inform the right people throughout the project.

- Your Stakeholder Assessment and Communication Plan should be updated periodically throughout the project. If the project is three months or less, it would probably be a one-off exercise at the start of the project. Longer projects warrant a periodic update.

- You can show how stakeholders' influence and involvement will change as the project proceeds from one stage to the next. This helps visualise project activity from a stakeholder perspective.

oooOooo

7| Evaluating Stakeholder Management Effectiveness

The two key aspects to evaluating effectiveness are learning from the past and using this to generate improvements for the future.

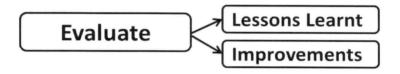

Typically, the evaluation of your stakeholder management process is not done as a separate activity but as part of the Lessons Learnt Review at the end of the project. However, very large projects, that have a dedicated stakeholder engagement team, may well conduct a separate lessons learnt exercise.

What to Cover in a Review

Stakeholder Management Effectiveness Review Template

Practical Project Stakeholder Management

Here is an example template that you can use as part of your stakeholder management review:

Project Stakeholder Management Process Evaluation

Project Name:
Project Manager: **Project Sponsor:**
Duration (start – end):   **Today's Date:**

Contributors to this Evaluation:

Place an "X" in the appropriate box to the right of each question.

1. Did we identify all the relevant stakeholders?	Yes, all	Most, minor missing	Most, Some Key missing	Several missing
2. Did we correctly assess the stakeholders?	Yes, completely	Mostly	Partially	Very Poorly
3. Did we effectively engage the stakeholders?	Yes, very well	Reasonably well	Not so well	Very poorly

Key Strengths of the Stakeholder Management Process	Key Weaknesses in the Stakeholder Management Process	Recommended Improvements to Future Stakeholder Management Processes

The first set of boxes provides a quick assessment on whether:

- we identified all the relevant stakeholders on the project;
- we correctly assessed the stakeholders in terms of their interest, involvement, impact, influence, support, expectation and needs; and
- we effectively engaged the stakeholders throughout the project life cycle.

The discussion and insights that support this quick assessment should be written in the table below the assessment.

- Key strengths of the process – these should be repeated on future projects.

| 50

Practical Project Stakeholder Management

- Key weaknesses in the process – these should be avoided on future projects.
- Recommended improvements for future stakeholder management processes.

This document can be discussed and completed during a final lessons learnt project meeting, or could be modified and emailed out to the key stakeholders requesting their input.

Not only is this a quick and simple way of evaluating effectiveness… it also is a very useful planning tool for the *next* project. On longer projects, you would perform your Project Lessons Learnt periodically throughout the project, including a Stakeholder Management Effectiveness assessment. This is to ensure that the current live project can benefit from focused improvements to the way stakeholders are engaged.

Chapter 7 Key Points

- As part of evaluating the project, it is important to evaluate the effectiveness of the stakeholder management process.
- You can use the template provided as a team assessment, or modify it for individual stakeholders to complete and return for evaluation.
- On very large projects, there is likely to be a separate Stakeholder Engagement role that supports the Project Manager; on smaller projects, this is done by the Project Manager. The way you go about evaluating stakeholder management effectiveness will depend upon the size and complexity of the project.

oooOooo

8| Ten Best Practices for Effective Project Stakeholder Management

If you've read chapters 1 through 7, you should have a good grasp of a professional project stakeholder management approach. You should now you have the knowledge and tools you need to perform an appropriate degree of stakeholder management on your projects. Below are 10 best practices to keep you purposeful in your stakeholder management.

1. **Take time to understand your stakeholders.** The more you understand what's important to them, their concerns and their needs, the better positioned you are to collaborate with them and for them to support you.

2. **Meet with your stakeholders early on in the project.** Relationship building takes time. When people only know you from your emails, it is very difficult for them to identify with you and support you on your project. As far as is practically possible, set up meetings with your key project stakeholders early on in the project.

3. **Involve them at the right time during the project life cycle.** Involvement automatically creates engagement. The more people are involved in something, they more they will support it. On large projects, you cannot involve everyone on the project in every discussion – it would be a practical impossibility. So it is important in your planning and early discussions to clarify when to involve the relevant people in relevant project activities.

4. **Keep them updated on project status.** Keep your project stakeholders up to date with project

progress, especially on tasks that affect them or their teams. At the same time, do not overburden your stakeholders with too much information that is irrelevant to them.

5. **Tailor your communication.** Different stakeholders have different "stakes" in the project. In our example, the Health and Safety manager has different interests to the Help Desk manager. So ensure your reporting to them and meetings with them is tailored to what they need, and want, to know.

6. **Adopt a "no surprises" culture on the project.** If you are aware of an issue or a risk that may negatively impact one or more stakeholders, let them know early on so that they have the time to make decisions and take corrective action.

7. **Tailor the process to fit your project.** The process I have described in this book can be very detailed and rigorous if you take all the steps and complete all the templates. The size, significance and complexity of your project should dictate the level of detail and effort you put into the assessment and documentation.

8. **You can't be all things to all people all of the time – prioritise.** On large projects, with many stakeholder individuals and groups, it is very difficult to ensure that everyone is fully engaged in the project. It could become a full time pre-occupation trying to keep all of the people happy all of the time... and we don't have the luxury of time on most projects. This is why the assessment is so important – engage those key stakeholders who need your time and attention the most.

9. **Update your assessment and engagement plans on long projects.** As the project

progresses, and the stakeholder involvement changes, the project dynamics change. Ensure you are tuned in to those changes from a stakeholder perspective.

10. **Build and re-enforce trust.** Each of the above nine points are important, but building and re-enforcing *trust* is the most important. You build trust by being interested, sincere, professional, honest and credible in all your dealings with people. Without trust, relationships fail. And with failed relationships, you lose collaboration and engagement on your project.

Concluding Remarks

In addition to what you have learnt in this book, I recommend that you brush up on your influencing and negotiation skills. There are a host of books and training courses on influencing and negotiation – my recommendation would be to attend a course that provides you with role-play opportunities to practice skills learnt.

Many project managers don't bother with stakeholder management formally, as they feel they don't have the time. Not taking a more considered approach to stakeholder management could save you time early in your project, but could also cost you much more time later... if not project failure.

As I mentioned earlier, the *spirit* of this process is not about the documentation produced. It's about taking the *actions* needed to help you better understand your stakeholders, and engage with them in a meaningful and collaborative way throughout the project life cycle. Using a formal Stakeholder Management approach will help you build *stronger* relationships and develop mutual trust on your projects.

Stakeholder management benefits all parties, with the overall aim of delivering successful projects.

oooOooo

About the Author: Emanuela Giangregorio

A multi-disciplinary, multi-industry, multi-national consultant.

I am a performance improvement consultant with over twenty years' practice delivering bespoke business training, coaching, team building and management consulting. I am South African with Italian heritage, based in the UK, and practice internationally.

I help organisations, teams and individuals be better at what they do, leading to greater fulfilment of personal and organisational goals.

I have written and delivered training programmes in generalist and specialist fields, including topics on strategic leadership, project management, change management, virtual collaboration, and personal effectiveness.

I am tenaciously results-focused, and engage individuals and teams with real-world practical experience, energy, enthusiasm and passion for continuous improvement.

oooOooo

Printed in Great Britain
by Amazon